PASSPORT SPAIN

Passport To The World

Passport Argentina
Passport Brazil
Passport China
Passport France
Passport Germany
Passport Hong Kong
Passport India
Passport Indonesia
Passport Israel
Passport Italy
Passport Japan
Passport Korea
Passport Mexico
Passport Philippines
Passport Russia
Passport Singapore
Passport South Africa
Passport Taiwan
Passport Thailand
Passport United Kingdom
Passport USA
Passport Vietnam

PASSPORT SPAIN

Your Pocket Guide to Spanish Business, Customs & Etiquette

Himilce Novas
Rosemary E. Silva

Passport Series Editor: Barbara Szerlip

WORLD TRADE PRESS®
Professional Books for International Trade

World Trade Press
1505 Fifth Avenue
San Rafael, California 94901 USA
Tel: (415) 454-9934
Fax: (415) 453-7980
E-mail: WorldPress@aol.com

"Passport to the World" concept: Edward G. Hinkelman
Cover design: Peter Jones/Marge Wilhite
Illustrations: Tom Watson

Library of Congress Cataloging-in-Publication Data
Novas, Hilmilce and Silva, Rosemary E.
Passport Spain: your pocket guide to Spanish business, customs & etiquette / Himilce Novas & Rosemary E. Silva
p. cm. -- (Passport to the world)
Includes bibliographical references.
ISBN 1-885073-35-6
1. Corporate culture -- Spain. 2. Business etiquette -- Spain. 3. Industrial management -- Social aspects -- Spain. 4. Negotiation in business -- Spain. 5. Intercultural communication. I. Title. II. Series.
HD58.7.S559 1996
390'.00946 -- dc21
96-52741 CIP

Printed in the United States of America

Table of Contents

SPAIN

A Rising European Star

Spain
Quick Look

Official name	Kingdom of Spain
Land area	504,784 sq km (194,897 sq mi)
Capital & largest city	Madrid, 2.9 million
Elevations	Highest – Mulhacén 3,478 m (11,411 ft) Lowest – sea level along coasts
People	
Population (1996)	39,887,240
Density	1 person per 77.6 sq km
Distribution (1990)	78.4% urban, 21.6% rural
Annual growth (1996)	0.3%
Official language	Castilian Spanish (and Catalan, Gallego and Euskera in their respective regions)
Major religions	Roman Catholicism 94.9%
Economy	
GDP (1994)	US$483 billion US$12,331 per capita
Foreign trade (1994)	Imports — US$92.7 billion Exports — US$73.5 billion
Principal trade partners	EU 75% USA 5%
Currency	Peseta (1 pta = 100 centimes)
Exchange rate (3/97)	142.7 ptas = US$1
Education and health	
Literacy (1991)	97%
Universities (1994)	1,415
Hospital beds (1991)	1 per 234 persons
Physicians (1991	1 per 257 persons
Life expectancy (1995)	Women — 81 years Men — 75 years
Infant mortality (1995)	6.7 per 1,000 live births

SPAIN

1 Country Facts

Geography & Demographics

Spain, the second largest country in Europe after France, takes its name from *Spania,* a Carthaginian word meaning "land of the rabbits." The country occupies about five-sixths of the Iberian Peninsula (the remainder constitutes Portugal, the microstate of Andorra, and the British possession of Gibraltar), as well as the Balearic Islands in the Mediterranean, the Canary Islands in the Atlantic, the enclaves of Ceuta and Melilla in northern Morocco, and three island groups off the coast of Morocco. Most of peninsular Spain is situated on a vast, high central plateau (the Meseta Central) that's crisscrossed and flanked by mountain ranges — the most famous being the majestic, snow-crested Pyrenees to the north, which separate the Iberian Peninsula from France and the rest of Europe.

Spain is endowed with 3,144 kilometers of coastline. The west coast (which is interrupted by Portugal) and the southwestern coast are bounded by the Atlantic Ocean, while the northwestern coast is washed by the Bay of Biscay. Spain's eastern and southeastern coasts look out onto the Mediterranean. The country's southernmost point is a mere 12 miles from the African continent, which lies across the Strait of Gibraltar.

Spaniards, who have among their forbears the Phoenicians, Greeks, Carthaginians, Romans, Celts, Iberians, Visigoths, Moors and Jews, are one of Europe's most diverse peoples. Many regions of the country are inhabited by ethnic groups which, with their own distinct customs and languages, have sometimes aspired to full independence.

In an effort to mollify such strong separatist sentiments, Spain's Constitution of 1978 called for the creation of 17 autonomous regions, each with its own legislature, capital and flag. Those regions are: Andalusia, Aragon, Asturias, the Balearic Islands, the Basque Country, the Canary Islands, Cantabria, Castile La Mancha, Castile and León, Catalonia, Valencia, Extremadura, Galicia, La Rioja, Comunidad de Madrid, Murcia and Navarre.

Climate

Spain has three distinct climatic zones. The northern coastal region is temperate with mild winters and cool summers. The skies are cloudy throughout the year, especially in Galicia. The soggy Galician town of Santiago de Compostela records the highest rainfall in Spain, with 1637 millimeters (64.5 inches) annually (three times more than London).

The Mediterranean coast of Catalonia and Valencia, the lowlands of Andalusia, and the Balearic Islands enjoy a Mediterranean climate. Winters are mild and occasionally rainy, while the summers are sunny and dry.

The interior of Spain experiences the most extreme fluctuations in temperature, with harsh winters and intensely hot and dry summers. Rain comes in spring and autumn, but not in sufficient quantity to quench the arid landscape. Once or twice annually, "Sahara rains" (which contain Sahara sand) stain everything a shade of pink.

The Canary Islands, a prime winter getaway destination for Europeans, have the country's steadiest climate, with temperatures that hover around 68°F (20°C) year-round. There's very little change in the weather pattern between night and day or between summer and winter.

Business Hours

Normal business hours are Monday through Friday 9 A.M. to 8 P.M. and Saturdays 9 A.M. to 1:30 P.M. (Government agencies have hours from 9 A.M. to 1 P.M. weekdays.) The hours of 1:30 P.M. to 4 P.M. are taken up by the *siesta,* when Spaniards go home or to restaurants for the midday meal and a bit of relaxation. It's becoming increasingly common for businesses to remain open during *siesta* hours. In the hottest months of July and August, when most Spaniards take their annual 30-day paid vacation, the workday follows the summer schedule (*horario de verano*) of 8:30 A.M. to 2:30 or 3 P.M.

Banking hours are from 8:30 or 9 A.M. to 2 or 2:30 P.M. on weekdays and from 9 A.M. to 1 P.M. on Saturdays. During the summer months most banks are closed Saturdays. Department stores and shops are generally open weekdays from 9 A.M. to 1:30 P.M. and from 5 P.M. to 8 P.M. A few remain open during the *siesta,* and many have hours on Saturdays (either a half or full day). Nearly all are closed on Sundays.

National Holidays

New Year's Day . . . . January 1
Epiphany . . . . January 6
Celebrates the coming of the Magi to Bethlehem
Carnival . . . . February or early March
Ends on or after Ash Wednesday with the Burial of the Sardine, a symbol of winter
Feast of San Jose . . . . March 19
National holy day of obligation
Holy Week (*Semana Santa*) . . . . the week leading up to Easter
May Day (Labor Day) . . . . May 1
Corpus Christi . . . . June (date varies)
Nationwide processions, the most elaborate in Sitges and Toledo
St. John's Day . . . . June 24
John the Baptist honored with night-long bonfires, especially along Mediterranean coast
Assumption Day . . . . August 15
Hispanic Day . . . . October 12
Commemorates Columbus' discovery of America
All Saints' Day . . . . November 1
Families place flowers on graves of their forbears
Constitution Day . . . . December 6
Celebrates ratification of Spain's 1978 constitution
Feast of the Immaculate Conception . . . . December 8
Begins the Christmas season
Christmas . . . . December 25

If a holiday falls on a Tuesday or Thursday, many people will take off the Monday or Friday in between to enjoy a long weekend, called a *puente* (bridge); many offices close.

(For more on holidays, see Chapter 16: Customs.)

2 The Spanish

Language

Spanish is basically of Latin origin, though many words that begin with *f* in other Romance languages begin with *h* (such as *hijo*, son), and the Moorish influence is seen in the many words starting with *al-* (like *algodón*, cotton). As with British and American English, the vocabulary sometimes changes on different sides of the ocean. (For example, peach is *melocoton* in Spain, while in Latin America it's *durazno*.)

The Castilian dialect, Castellano, is the accepted standard. The spelling system and pronunciation are in strict accord, with only a few exceptions. Thus, once Spanish letters and their sounds are mastered, it's simple to pronounce newly encountered words. Castilian Spanish has absorbed a number of words from American English, such as *windsurfista* (windsurfer) and *Walkman*. English words of Spanish origin include: *cargo, hacienda, patio, armada, guerilla, junta, plaza, canyon, rodeo, adobe, vanilla, armadillo, tornado, embargo* and *bonanza*. The term *fifth column*, as in secret enemy sympathizers who work as spies or saboteurs, was coined during the Spanish Civil War. In 1936, General Emilio Mola advanced on Madrid with a four-column army. "The fifth column," he announced over the radio, "is within the city."

While most Spaniards speak Castilian, the Basques of the north, the Catalans of the far northeast, and the Galicians of the northwest are also fluent in their own regional languages — Euskera, Catalan and Gallego respectively.

Euskera (a.k.a. Basque) is believed to have evolved before the Romans arrived in Spain; it's unique in that it's the only non-Indo-European language of western Europe. Despite many efforts, its origin has never been linked to any other language. Prior to the 20th century, it was spoken mainly by country folk (on both sides of the Spanish-French border). In 1978, after being proclaimed the official language of Basque Country, it was transformed into a medium for literature and journalism. The traditional Basque sport of jai alai — a high-speed court game played with a ball and curved wicker baskets strapped to the wrist — takes it name from the Basque words for *joyous* and *festival*. (For more on jai alai, see Chapter 20.)

Catalan (spoken in the Balearic Islands, Andorra and Valencia, as well as in Catalonia) is related to Provençal, once the language of the French troubadours. It's come to play an increasingly important role in business, because Spain's second largest city and biggest port — Barcelona, in the heart of Catalonia — is a vital center for commerce. Of Barcelona's five daily newspapers, two are in Catalan, and one of three Barcelona public TV stations broadcasts in Catalan exclusively. Those with a knowledge of Spanish can recognize Catalan words by the consonant clusters tg, ts, tx, tz and ny, and by the frequent use of the letter x.

Gallego (a.k.a. Galician) is the ancestor of modern Portuguese. In the 14th century, it was displaced by Castilian but kept alive in the countryside. Then, in the late 19th century, Gallego was the focus of a literary revival that continues to this day.

More than mere dialects, regional languages are afforded equal status with Castilian in their regions, and they remain at the forefront of an ongoing domestic debate over autonomy and separatism. A small minority of Spaniards speak their regional language exclusively. Some Spaniards, particularly in the big cities, speak British English, and a good number are conversant in French or Portuguese.

The Heavy Hand of Catholicism

In 711, Muslims (Moors) from North Africa crossed the Strait of Gibraltar into Spain, and within a decade, they'd conquered almost the entire Iberian Peninsula. Various Christian kingdoms arose, but it wasn't until the 11th century that they managed to force the Moors into retreat. Then, in 1469, the royal marriage of Ferdinand of Aragon (age 17) and Isabella of Castile united their respective kingdoms, which were the country's largest. In 1480, these two "Catholic Kings," as the Pope called them, established the Inquisition, a tribunal whose job was to achieve national religious unity and a purity of faith.

All Jews (many of whom held high advisory positions in the courts) and Moors (who had created the irrigation systems that made Spain's orchards and exotic gardens possible) were forced to either convert or emigrate, under penalty of death. Those who abandoned Islam for the cross were called *moriscos*. *Marranos* professed Christianity in order to remain in their homeland but practiced Judaism in secret. Some 400,000 other Jews fled the country; a variety of Spanish known as Ladino is still spoken in

Turkey and Israel by their descendants. Countless false converts, as well as Protestants, were tortured until they confessed to heresy, then imprisoned, hanged, beheaded or burned at the stake in elaborate *autos-da-fé* (acts of faith), staged to remind the populace of the terrors of the Last Judgment.

The Inquisition held sway for several hundred years and its legacy for even longer. Throughout the 19th and much of the 20th centuries, the government continued to suppress all forms of worship other than Roman Catholicism. Paradoxically, many Jews found asylum from Hitler's Final Solution in Spain during Franco's Fascist regime. But until 1967, when the Law on Religious Freedom was passed, Protestants and Jews were still forbidden to conduct religious services or hold public office.

Today, about 95 percent of the populace is Roman Catholic, but long gone are the days when everyone flocked to church on Sunday. Still, the observance of holy days remains an important aspect of life. Many partake for the sheer pageantry and communal enjoyment.

The Spanish Civil War & The Rise of Franco

The Spanish Civil War (1936-1939) was actually three wars — one between traditionalists and liberal reformers (the latter wanted free elections, free press and lay education), one between the more economically advanced parts of the country and government control from Madrid, and one between an aspiring working class and a self-absorbed landowning upper class. For the first time in history, the bombing of civilians on a large scale was used as a terror tactic. The conflict eventually resulted in about 100,000 deaths in battle, 10,000 in air raids, 220,000 murders and executions, 50,000 deaths from starvation and disease, and the permanent exile of another 350,000. In the end, it left Spain exhausted, bitter and greatly damaged. And it served as an ominous preview of World War II, pitching Nazi Germany and Fascist Italy against Soviet Russia.

In 1936, Spain was polarized between its orthodox Republican government and the left Socialists, who wished to establish a "dictatorship of the proletariat." The murder of the leader of the extreme right touched off both a military uprising and a social revolution. The working class took over many factories and farms were collectivized.

Generalissimo Francisco Franco was in charge of the core of the Nationalist (Republican) Army, and he needed help. When France and Britain refused to intervene, he turned to Hitler (who provided tanks, artillery and 100 combat planes) and Mussolini (who provided tanks, artillery and ground troops). On April 26, 1937, German planes bombed the civilian town of Guernica, resulting in international outrage and the inspiration for one of Pablo Picasso's most famous paintings. Franco transferred his efforts to this area and began a series of victories that led to the war's end — and to a political regime that would hold Spain in a kind of time-warp for more than a generation.

Isolation & Absolute Power

Throughout his 36-year rule, Franco's authority was based on the emergency powers he'd been granted by his fellow generals during the war. He implemented brutal censorship of the press and of political expression in general, gave the church control over education, cut his country off from the international marketplace, and did little to alleviate the extreme division between rich and poor. The 1940s were years of economic stagnation, near famine, and the black market; and his policies (which forbade labor unions and included having officials and military personnel use the Fascist salute on ceremonial occasions) resulted in Spain being excluded from the original United Nations roster (a decision that was reversed ten years later).

As recently as 1960, almost 13 percent of the population was considered illiterate, some factory workers were surviving on 36 pesetas (US$0.60) a day, and censorship of outside events remained such that a high court judge in Madrid first heard of the Holocaust at the time of Eichmann's trial in 1961. Still, Franco continued to be admired by many for maintaining the country's longest period of stability in centuries. "Africa begins at the Pyrenees" goes an old Spanish adage, and that isolation was to continue until Franco's death in 1975. Only then would Spain finally be free to catch up, economically, technologically and otherwise, with the rest of Europe.

Family

The family is the backbone of Spanish society, providing a social and economic support system. Relatives commonly live in the same city, often just a short distance from each other, or even in the same apartment building. Three generations often live under one roof, though this practice isn't quite as common as it used to be. Family members are depended on to perform tasks like baby-sitting or caring for the sick. Young Spaniards usually live at home until they're well into their twenties or have married. *Vive de tus padres hasta que puedas vivir de tus hijos* (Live off your parents until you can live off your children) goes a Spanish expression.

Spain's business culture is structured to honor such familial ties and obligations. New fathers are granted several days paternity leave, and new mothers enjoy three-months' paid maternity leave. And as long as their children are too young to attend school, mothers may leave work an hour early each day.

The Grandee Spirit Lives On

As in most of Europe, class distinctions are heavily underscored. The Spanish aristocracy is still going strong. On any given day, titles are being sought after or inherited and blood lines touted. Because the country's monied elite was idle from the 15th through 18th centuries, a general disdain of manual labor developed on the part of the middle and upper classes that still exists today. Thus, a middle-class Spaniard would never take a manual job such as waitressing, even to earn some extra cash.

Traditionally, upper-crust Spaniards (referred to pejoratively as *pijos* — spoiled rich kids) have enjoyed the greatest access to positions of power and influence in the government, the military, finance, business and the church. (See Chapter 6: Enchufe = Nepotism.) Nowadays, the lower and middle classes enjoy greater mobility. Still, there are limits. Spain's top corporate executives are almost exclusively upper class, and they're wooed by foreign companies for their contacts with Spain's well-heeled and influential citizenry.

Along with a rigid class structure, but not contrary to it, exists *individualismo*, the notion every Spaniard has that he or she is unique and even morally superior to the next person, regardless of wealth and position in society.

National Identity and Pride

Spaniards take pride in their ability to balance

work and leisure, act spontaneously and live in the moment (*"Un día es un día,"* as they say), remain persistent in the face of challenge, and bend the rules and negotiate in order to achieve a desired effect. And they consider themselves to be a kind, generous and tolerant people.

They're proud to be descended from the Iberians, an ancient people who were invaded by the Carthaginians, Celts, Romans, Vandals, Visigoths and Moors, all of whom contributed to Spain's rich, multilayered culture. Spain boasts one of the oldest cities in Europe, Cádiz, founded by the Phoenicians in 1100 B.C., as well as such architectural treasures as the Roman aqueduct at Segovia and the Alhambra palace in Granada (one of the finest examples of Moorish architecture in Europe).

Spain was the birthplace of some of the world's greatest artists, among them El Greco, Diego Rodríguez de Silva Velázquez, Bartolomé Estaban Murillo, Francisco Jose de Goya, Pablo Picasso, Juan Gris, Joan Miró and Salvador Dalí (the Dalí Museum is second in popularity only to Madrid's Prado); composers Isaac Manuel Francisco Albéniz, Enrique Granados and Manuel de Falla; cellist Pablo Casals; opera singers Monserrat Caballé and Jose Carreras; and popular singer Julio Iglesias.

Literary landmarks include the 13th-century epic poem "Cantar de Mio Cid" (The Poem of the Cid), the poems of Federico Garcia Lorca and the novels of Nobel-prize author Camilo José Cela (*Mazurka for Two Dead*). And of Miguel de Cervantes' *Don Quixote de la Mancha*, first published in 1605, British critic Alastair Reid has written, "It is the most profound study ever made of the Spanish character ... an achievement so towering as to be safely unsurpassable, nothing more or less than the greatest book in the world."

One of the most innovative architects of the 20th century, "that mad Catalan" Antonio Gaudí, earned recognition for creating a fantastic, surrealistic style that incorporated elements from Moorish, Gothic and Art Nouveau and that predated Surrealism by some forty years. Gaudí's fragmented tile work is believed to have inspired Pablo Picasso's cubist paintings. His masterpiece, the Church of the Sagrada Família in Barcelona, was begun in 1903. In 1936, a decade after Gaudí's death, it was set afire by anarchists, and all design records were destroyed. Despite the efforts of a half dozen architects since then, the church remains unfinished.

Filmmakers Luis Buñuel (*The Andalusian Dog, Discreet Charm of the Bourgeoisie*) and Pedro Almodóvar (*Woman on the Verge of a Nervous Breakdown*) enjoy a global cinematic following. Pilar Miró (*Gary Cooper, Who Art in Heaven*) is one of the few women in Spanish film to rise to the top.

Attitudes Toward Other Cultures

Due to the efforts of explorers like Hernán Cortés, Francisco Pizarro, Hernando de Soto, Cabeza de Vaca and Vasco Nuñez de Balboa (who named the very unpacific Pacific Ocean), Spain colonized most of the Americas in the 16th century, from Florida and the California coast to the tip of South America, as well as the Philippines, thus enjoying one of the greatest empires in history. Today, Spain and many of its former colonies are tied not only by a common language and cultural heritage, but also by mutual good will. Spain is committed to defending Latin American interests in Venezuela, Argentina, Bolivia, Uruguay, Chile, the Dominican Republic and elsewhere.

Though an integral part of Europe, Spaniards discern keen cultural difference between themselves and their neighbors. Most significantly, they view the French, English and Germans, as well as Americans and Asians, as workaholics who are unable to strike a healthy balance between labor and leisure and thus don't live life to its fullest.

As for North Americans:

- Many Spaniards hold fast to the stereotype that they're poorly informed about world cultures and history and therefore devalue tradition.
- American businesspeople are seen as being obsessed with details (*detallismo*), terrified of ambiguity, and wanting everything "nailed down." (Ironically, Americans like to think of themselves as being flexible.)
- Spaniards believe that the U.S. emphasis on rugged individualism and self-reliance has led to a breakdown of both the American family and its overall society.
- While U.S. ingenuity (especially technology) is admired, Americans are seen as a restless people who are never content with their accomplishments.

How Others View the Spanish

Most of the world views the Spanish as proud, energetic and fun-loving, and as dangerously aggressive drivers. They marvel at the Spaniards' ability to socialize until nearly dawn and then appear at work the next day completely refreshed. Americans, and some Europeans, believe that the Spanish are much too laissez-faire in their habits and that as a result, they leave too much to chance.

The world also views Spain as a country that has come into its own in the wake of Franco's dictatorship. Spain's membership in NATO and its entrance into the European Economic Council in

1986 confirmed its transformation, within an extraordinarily brief period, from the second poorest nation in Western Europe to a thriving capitalist economy. Spain's role as host to the 1992 Olympic Summer Games and the 1992 World's Fair has also added to its image as a rising European star.

3 Cultural Stereotypes

Party Animals

Spaniards dedicate too much time to the pursuit of leisure.

The truth is that Spaniards work just as long, and in some cases longer, than other peoples, but they divide their workday differently in reverence to the age-old *siesta* tradition. The average Spaniard works 8.5 hours a day, five days a week, plus half a day on Saturday. In July and August, many work an abbreviated schedule (from about 8:30 A.M. to 3 P.M.), then go home to escape the heat. However, once the official workday comes to a close, few stay late to finish up a project or to put in extra hours, unless a terrible crisis has befallen the company.

Business is often conducted over dinner, and on some nights, especially in summer, Spaniards may stay out until the wee hours. Most retire at a fairly normal hour. However, they won't pass up an opportunity to spend time with family and friends just because they're worried about getting enough rest to be effective at work the next day.

It may appear to foreigners that the Spanish are leisure driven because cafes, restaurants, theaters, nightclubs, discos, stores and sidewalks seem always to bustle with activity. (Spaniards rarely sit down to dinner before 9 P.M., and most restaurants are still packed at 11 P.M.) One's home is reserved for family and close friends; Spaniards seek out public venues when meeting for business or simply for long, leisurely hours of conversation and gossip. They also tend to spend their spare time out in the world, rather than in front of a television set. (For more on this, see Chapter 20: Socializing.)

Not Ambitious

Spaniards have no desire to better themselves or their country.

Spaniards have a very strong work ethic. In fact, they often hold down two jobs at once (because of modest salaries and a high cost of living) or combine work with study. The Catalans and Basques, in particular, have a reputation for their industriousness.

If ambition is measured by taking calculated risks (like changing professions or moving to another company in pursuit of better pay or intellectual challenges), Spaniards are likely to fall short. Job satisfaction is measured not only in terms of *pesetas* and personal growth, but also by the status that a job title affords and a person's history with a company. It's of the utmost importance for Spaniards to preserve their public image, so they're more likely to wait for promotions (which, in Spain, are based on seniority or loyalty, as well as achievement) than move to another company, where they may have to start in a low position in the chain of command. (For more on this, see Chapter 6: The Work Environment.)

Overly Emotional

Spaniards are excitable and fly off the handle easily.

Spaniards speak with dramatic flair. What may appear "emotional" to a foreigner is perfectly natural to them. Spaniards also tend to speak loudly and to constantly interrupt each other, not out of rudeness or anger but to show that they're interested. They're also fond of superlatives. When disagreements in professional situations occur, Spaniards raise their voices even louder — not to vent frustration but as a way of restating their position.

4 Regional Differences

Ethnic nationalism runs deep. In fact, most Spaniards identify first and foremost with their autonomous region and only then with the nation as a whole. Franco's death brought an end to a long ban on the expression of cultural diversity. Regional governments encourage ethnic pride by emphasizing their particular language, arts and traditions. Some Spaniards, however, assert that regional nationalism is detrimental to progress and that at a time when Europe is coming together as a community, Spain should unite more strongly.

Of the country's 17 autonomous groupings, the 5 with the most political and economic influence are the Andalusians, the Castilians, the Basques, the Catalans and the Galicians.

The Andalusians

Andalusians, who inhabit the largest and most populated of Spain's autonomous regions, have a reputation for being spontaneous and charming. The region's thriving silicon chip industry has earned it the sobriquet "California of Spain." Andulusia is also a major source of agricultural products (including wine, cork and olive oil), though it's struggling to recover from the century's worst drought.

The Castilians

The Castilians inhabit Spain's heartland (Castile-La Mancha, Castile, Leon and Comunidad de Madrid) and are viewed by their fellow countrymen as gracious, proud, individualistic and rather stubborn. Castilians are known for their skills in administration, a tradition that is many centuries old. In 1560, under the auspices of Felipe II, Madrid — originally the Moorish village of Madjrit — became the nation's administrative hub. Nowadays, Madrid is the country's largest urban center and the locus for commerce, finance, retail and transportation, as well as the headquarters for various international companies. *Madrileños* are known for their ambition, intensity and generosity.

The Basques

Basque Country *(Euzkardi)* consists of three provinces along the Bay of Biscay and part of Navarre. Its inhabitants are ethnically distinct not only from other Spaniards but from all Europeans, and they've managed to retain their distinctiveness through millennia. As the saying goes: *Before God was God and boulders were boulders, the Basques were already Basques.*

Since its founding in 1959, the small Basque terrorist group called ETA or *Euskadi ta Askatasuna* (Basque Homeland and Freedom) has attempted to secure complete independence for the Basque Country through intimidation and violence (usually guns and bombs). Since 1968, the ETA has allegedly been responsible for more than 750 deaths (members of the government, the military and security forces; moderate Basques; and, in early 1997, a top Madrid judge) and for untold millions of dollars worth of property damage. The government has tried through various means (negotiations, counter-terrorist operations) to bring an end to this, its trickiest regional problem, but without success.

Most Basques deplore ETA terrorism, and they haven't let it hamper their region's economic development. The Basques are currently Spain's leading producer of advanced technology and engineering systems, they have huge capital investments and a booming aerospace sector, and they're highly involved in export markets. It's one of the few regions that outperforms the country as a whole; in 1995, its GNP rose 3.9 percent, compared with 2.9 percent overall. Bilbao is the busiest Spanish port.

The Catalans

The Catalans view themselves as more European than Spanish, and they're quick to note that Catalonia belonged to Charlemagne, not the Moors. Franco's ban of the Catalan language, the Catalonia flag, and even the *sardana* (the traditional Catalan dance) fueled nationalist sentiment. (The word *xarnego* has come to mean any working-class non-Catalan who lives in Catalonia — and it's used pejoratively.) Like the Basques, they've been vocal about independence but to a lesser degree.

Catalans are viewed by their fellow countrymen as practical, industrious and as having extraordinary business acumen. Though only 13 percent of Spain's populace lives here, Catalonia accounts for nearly one-fifth of the GDP, a quarter of total exports, nearly two-fifths of industrial exports, and it's home to 1,400 foreign investors. Barcelona is Spain's most developed industrial and commercial center and one of Europe's largest Mediterranean ports.

The Galicians

The Galicians are looked upon by their fellow Spaniards as hardworking and thrifty. They're also thought to suffer from sentimentality and melancholy (*morriña*), like the Irish who share their Celtic roots. (Not coincidentally, their favorite instrument is the bagpipes.) Galicia is home to one of Europe's most technologically advanced factory fishing fleets, and it supplies the country with about one-third of its fish. (Spaniards consume 80 pounds of fish per person annually, more than any other European population except the Portuguese.) Galicians are the poorest of all Spaniards. For many centuries, the threat of poverty has forced many of them to move to other parts of Spain or to emigrate to South America and, more recently, to other countries in Europe.

Gitanos

One ethnic minority with no region to call home are Spain's half million gypsies (*gitanos*), who probably arrived (via Africa) in about 1425 and have been subject to extreme prejudice ever since. They quickly became known as beggars, caravan vagabonds, fortune-tellers, thieves, horse traders, dancers, blacksmiths and knife sharpeners.

In 1558, King Philip II ordered them to abandon their "wild life" and settle. In 1633, Philip IV forbade them to wear traditional clothing, speak their own language, or dance their *zarabandas* (which were, wrote one church Father, "so lewd in words and so detestable in movement that they make decent people blush"). He also ordered them to be "taken from their places of habitation, separated from one another, with express prohibition to come together publicly or in secret ... under penalty of three years banishment."

In 1692, Charles II forbade the *gitanos* to carry weapons of any kind, to own horses, to have any occupation other than agriculture, or to leave their villages — the latter crime punishable by six years forced labor in a ship's galley. Local magistrates were authorized to open fire on them as "public bandits" should they refuse to surrender their arms and to pursue them even into refuge churches, which were open to all criminals and considered sacrosanct. Things improved somewhat in the 18th century. Charles III dubbed them "neo-Castilians," allowed them to return to their traditional trades, and even threw a few new ones their way, including bullfighting, shoeblacking and animal slaughtering.

But despite such a difficult history, a good number of *gitanos* have managed to enter mainstream Spanish life; some have even been elected to parliament and created political organizations like the Union of the Gypsy People. Still, most remain on the fringes of society. Illiterate and impoverished, they inhabit encampments, shantytowns and squalid apartment buildings primarily in the south, Madrid and Barcelona. They scrounge for a living washing car windshields, trading in outdoor markets, selling lottery tickets, stealing and begging. Government efforts to provide them with decent housing, educations and job training have been largely unsuccessful.

5 Government & Business

Business occupies a position of privilege in Spanish society. In the 22 years since Franco's death, the government has shown a strong commitment to social and economic modernization, which was a prerequisite for Spain's entry into the European Union (EU). In order to meet Maastricht Treaty criteria for admission into the EU's single currency European Monetary Union, however, it still has much to do about instituting welfare reform, privatization, deregulation and deficit reduction.

A critical factor in the country's success to date has been the encouragement of foreign investment. The 1991 Budget Act ensured EU enterprises the same treatment as local companies in strategic sectors such as TV and radio broadcasting, air transportation and gambling. In 1992, all existing foreign exchange and capital controls were abolished, giving residents and nonresidents complete freedom in financial transactions — including payments, receipts or transfers generated by foreign investments in Spain. That same year, the number of foreign investments previously requiring government authorization was decreased.

Barriers to Trade and Competition

Thanks to the center-right government of Jose María Aznar and the Popular Party, elected in March 1996 to replaced the Socialist leadership, trade barriers are falling rapidly. Prime Minister Aznar is committed to sweeping through economic reform packages designed to improve conditions for businesses.

In June, 1996, the government introduced four "decree" laws designed to dramatically reduce the tax burden on businesses in the short term (an estimated US$1.5 billion) and encourage economic growth and market confidence in the long run; liberalize key sectors of the economy (namely the land, energy, and telecommunications markets); eliminate price controls for some fuels; remove building restrictions (which could triple the amount of land on the market); encourage job creation; and restrict Spain's mighty professional guilds. The June laws also eliminated double taxation for many foreign companies doing business in Spain. (However, it should be noted that overly optimistic growth forecasts led to a deficit shortfall at the end of 1996, in response to which the government increased indirect taxes on alcohol and tobacco.)

This reform package sent a strong message that Spain has turned its back on the European welfare culture and embraced American-style competition. It's hoped that some of the corporations that bypassed Spain for Eastern Europe, Latin America, and Asia in the late 1980s and early 1990s will give Spain a second look.

While the Aznar government has opened the door to reform, it still needs to address the country's rigid labor legislation. There are, for example, severe restrictions on firing employees (and thus hiring new ones) and Spain has extremely high severance payments. This is tricky business, as the government doesn't want to strain relations with trade unions. Other issues that need attention are revamping the income tax system, cutting back on the high Social Security and redundancy rates that companies are required to pay (both of which are supported by the trade unions), and removing limits on competition in several sectors.

6 The Work Environment

Seniority = Status

Spanish businesses are run like autocracies or empires, wherein all the power is concentrated in the hands of one or a few. Workers are organized into highly compartmentalized ranks, each subordinate to the one above it. Status — in corporate environments, as well as elsewhere in society — is derived from an individual's position within the hierarchy, not from high performance or competence. Seniority counts for everything. It's the most critical factor in determining promotions, which in turn confer greater status and a better title. Some historians and cultural anthropologists attribute this hierarchical structure to the era when one's prestige was derived from being a *hidalgo* (literally, the son of).

Ambition, in the American sense, isn't a Spanish trait. While a U.S. businessperson might be impressed by someone's salary and professional accomplishments, a Spaniard would look to that person's title; he would be unlikely to give up a high-ranking position because the work wasn't challenging or the salary was inadequate. Thus, Spaniards are inclined to stay with a company and wait for the promotion they're bound to get, rather than to start over at another job — even if it's more interesting — and risk the loss of all the status they've accrued.

The Meaning of Success

Pride and honor take precedence over "the bottom line." A business with a centuries-old history and a traditional way of doing things is considered just as impressive as a new business with state-of-the-art management techniques and spectacular sales.

As many Spanish companies are both small and family-run, next year's goals are assumed to be the same as those of previous years. Change (bigger, better, faster) isn't necessarily aspired to when things have worked well enough in the past — an attitude summed up by the American colloquialism, "If it ain't broke, don't fix it."

Enchufe = Nepotism

Nepotism is commonplace, as Spaniards like to hire those they know they can trust. They depend on a whole network of personal relationships and are apt to hire *una persona de confianza* (a family member, friend or individual whose family's reputation they know) over a stranger — even if the stranger has more impressive credentials or business acumen. However, this system of networking, called *enchufe* (literally, an electric socket), is gradually giving way to a system of promotion by merit. If you don't have the benefit of such a network, it's much harder to become an insider and to get ahead.

Teamwork: Often a Problem

Employees in small- and medium-sized enterprises (about 88 percent of private-sector jobs) usually lack a formal business education. Instead, they hold college degrees in areas such as law, political science, economics or philosophy or have learned their skills on the job.

One result of this is that teamwork (from an American or Japanese perspective) is often lacking. On the other side of the equation, individuality (often a virtue in the U.S. workplace) and "healthy" competition (elsewhere believed to spur people on to do their best work) are viewed as potentially destructive.

The Spanish Work Ethic

Most Spaniards seek a balance between work and leisure. Employment is viewed as a way to make a living, not as a definition of who one is, and "workaholism" is rarely encountered. Spaniards find it a great waste for individuals to be so driven that they sacrifice fun, family and other fulfilling aspects of life.

Spaniards enjoy a much more relaxed pace at work than those in many other cultures. A few hours in the morning are taken up with reading the newspaper, chatting with colleagues, and possibly a half-hour breakfast break. Between 1:30 P.M. and 4 P.M. is *siesta*, time for a leisurely midday meal (it's unheard of to work through lunch or to eat hurriedly at one's desk), with the workday ending at 7 P.M. (except in summer, when many businesses shut down about 3 P.M.). Attempts to impose strict adherence to rules and schedules may be reminiscent to some workers of the Franco era. That having been said, the work ethic is more intense in the large cities and in the northern parts of the country.

Part of the reason the pace is more relaxed is that goal setting and personal achievement reap little reward in the workplace. Spaniards don't think that the way to better oneself is to work harder or longer. And Spain has such strong job protection laws that the chances of being fired are minimal. Trade unions are large, active and powerful. However, the *Estatuto del Trabajor* (Workers' Code) dictates employee job requirements and breaches can lead to docked pay or suspension.

In June and December, salaries are doubled. And if a company has reaped particularly high profits, those salaries may even triple. Other job benefits include an annual 30-day paid vacation (usually in August) and paid time-off for some 15 national holidays, as well as important local fiestas. There's a compulsory retirement age of 65. Employers aren't required to provide pensions.

Decision Making

The autocratic management style dictates that decisions rest in the hands of the top echelon and are never based on consensus. (Some historians have traced this back to the era of Queen Isabella and King Ferdinand, when power was concentrated at the top.) The highest-ranking individuals in the company review the reports of many different departments, but they don't depend on those lower in the chain of command for guidance. To do so would be a show of weakness and ineffectiveness.

Subordinates are discouraged from showing initiative or publicly expressing their opinions (as in a meeting). There are a number of reasons of this — out of respect for authority, for fear of looking foolish (*hacer el ridículo*), or out of cynicism about what may or may not be accomplished by their actions. Also, salary increases are often negotiated on a national basis once a year, and again, they're tied to one's status within the organization, not based on individual moxie. Added to this is the fact that in a tight job market (as of November, 1996, 22 percent of the labor force was without work), employers don't feel pressured to offer financial incentives. All this makes it difficult for talented and motivated individuals to excel.

If a decision impacting the internal affairs of an enterprise doesn't meet with widespread approval, employee protests will sometimes erupt. In such a case, the decision makers may give in to the pressure and go back to the table to modify their plan or policy.

The Mid-Level Manager

Since many businesses are family owned and operated, the hierarchy may not be readily apparent. Non-Spaniards may be under the impression that they're dealing with a decision maker, only to find out later that they're not. Though middle-level managers have no power to render a decision, non-Spaniards are advised to establish good relations with them, as they're the ones who'll prepare the reports on which decisions *will* be based.

The Internet

To date, Spain hasn't taken much advantage of the Internet as an international business tool.

In June 1996, Madrid was the site of the Fifth International Conference on Cyberspace — the first time the event was held in Europe. But the fact is that less than one percent of the populace uses the Internet, exorbitant rates being a primary factor. According to Telefónica de España's statistics, daily use averages 9.5 minutes for every 24 hours of capacity.

7 Women in Business

Traditional Roles

"What is most Spanish? The modesty of our women, not contaminated by feminism."

-- Jacinto Benavente y Martínez (1866-1954)

Queen Isabella I's reign (1474-1504) is credited with moving Spain into *el siglo de oro* (the golden century), an era of power and leadership in world affairs that would never be repeated. But four centuries later, after the death of King Ferdinand VII, Ferdinand's brother contested the right of Isabella II, the king's daughter, to succeed to the throne, based on the fact that she was female — a stance that set off the Carlist Wars. Isabella II did eventually get her crown, though the country was ruled by the army and her "insupportable" behavior (Isabella was allegedly a nymphomanic) led to her dethronement and exile in 1868.

As recently as the mid-19th century, 85 percent of Spanish women were illiterate. Even the well-to-do lived within cultural confines not dissimilar to purdah; what little education they received was via private tutors or the convent, both designed to turn out perfect, pious ladies but not well-rounded or intellectually curious ones. All (including queens) were expected to be obedient wives and mothers; most marriages were "arranged," with girls wedded early to men twice their age or older. For the unprivileged majority, there were few employment opportunities beyond agriculture, domestic service or grueling (and very unsafe) factory work. Though Primo de Rivera awarded his countrywomen municipal suffrage in 1924, it was of little use under his dictatorship.

"The Spanish mother," wrote one traveler of the era, "has no sympathy with the women in politics and very little with the bobbed-haired bathing girls with their cigarettes ... They are still content to play in a domestic drama of the Middle Ages ... living for the most part in a veiled world." A few managed to rise above such circumstances. One was Emilia Pardo Bazan, a novelist, essayist and critic who wrote graphically about the lives of *cigarillo* girls in the tobacco factories of her native Galicia. Another was Caroline "La Belle" Otero (1868-1965), a flamboyant dancer who rose from poverty to become one of Europe's most famous "grand horizontals," the consort of international royalty, and a multimillionaire. A number of women fought with the Loyalist militia during the Spanish Civil War in the 1930s, and communist Dolores Ibarruri, a.k.a. *La Pasionaria* (The Passionate One), was known for her stirring Civil War speeches, which she continued to give in exile in Russia.

It wasn't until 1926 that women's rights groups, like the Lyceum Club, were formed. Women's status improved with the 1931 Constitution, but many gains (like the right to initiate a divorce) were subsequently erased by Franco — who also forbade women to work outside their homes or to use contraceptives. (Until the mid-1970s, families of eight weren't uncommon.) Franco also instituted severe punishment for female (but not male) adultery.

In the wake of Franco's death, the 1978 Constitution was ratified, and it specifically prohibited gender discrimination, in the workplace and elsewhere. In the 1980s, contraception, abortion and divorce were legalized and the Women's Institute, a national equality commission, was created.

Trends

More and more Spanish women are pursuing careers, especially in the large cities like Madrid and Barcelona. They're well represented in business, law, medicine, science and education. In the corporate world, they've succeeded in establishing themselves in middle management but are generally still shut out of the top echelon. In certain regions (Catalonia, for example), women hold more prestigious jobs than in Madrid. As it is with men, class, educational status and connections are determining factors for success.

Still, the inequities remain readily apparent. "In theory, we have equal rights," explained Maria Pilar Marmol, secretary general of the Federation of Progressive Women, a leading feminist group, in 1993. "In reality, it's not 100 percent." In 1994, studies revealed that while women were entering virtually every profession, they were the most hurt by Spain's high unemployment. Men held two out of every three jobs, women's wages were 30 percent lower than men's, and women had to work harder than their male counterparts to get ahead. According to Cristina Sánchez (the most celebrated woman in Spanish bullfighting, an almost exclusively male domain), "You have to prove yourself or people will say it's because you're a woman that you failed." This seems to hold true for most women, regardless of their profession.

In the mid-1990s, Cristina Alberdi Alonso (Spain's Minister of Social Affairs) helped set in motion what's being called "a second feminist movement." Alonso is calling for greater job opportunities for women in middle management and above, an end to the typical portrayal of women as housewives in advertising, and the abolition of the term *señorita* to describe an unmarried woman. (All women should be called *señora,* Alonso believes, so that their marital status will be as private as it is for men.)

Machismo: Still Alive & Well

Spanish men tend to be very vocal, and often loud, when it comes to women, as the phrase *tortura de la galanteria* (the torture of compliments) suggests. However, *galanteria,* when taken too far, becomes harassment.

In a typical scenario, younger women walking alone on the street are bombarded with unwanted gestures, catcalls, comments and uncivilized advances. Such behavior was once common on every urban and rural corner of Spain, but now it seems confined to the more remote areas. The best way for women to cope is to remain alert and silent and to avoid eye contact. If the behavior persists or you're being pursued, seek out a policeman if possible, or any respectable-looking person on the street, and the problem will probably go away.

In 1996, the whole country — men and women alike — went into an uproar when, at ceremonies marking the 18th anniversary of the 1978 Constitution, Miguel Ángel Rodríguez (the Number Two man in the Spanish government) compared that document to a person reaching maturity by saying, "If it were a girl, it would put on a long dress." When the matter was discussed in Parliament a few weeks later, female legislators stormed out of the chamber in protest, denouncing Rodríguez's *machismo* as being out of step with the times.

Strategies for Businesswomen

Foreign businesswomen should encounter little if any resistance in pursuing their objectives, and they should expect to be included in all aspects of negotiations, including evening business activities.

A female team leader can make it abundantly clear that she's in charge by putting her name at the top of a team list and by emphasizing her credentials. She can be certain that Spaniards will show her the respect accorded men in high positions. Nonetheless, she may wish to instruct her team to:

- defer to her when questions are directed to others that would normally be put to the team leader
- refrain from disagreeing with her or amongst themselves, and
- refrain from engaging in "brainstorming" sessions in front of Spanish counterparts.

8 Making Connections

Relationships are Key

The success of most business ventures rests on developing good personal relationships. Spaniards don't like to conduct business with strangers. They need to know first and foremost that they're dealing with trustworthy individuals, and this sometimes takes precedence over the quality of products, services or their price (especially in large account sales). When reaching a decision, Spaniards weigh every aspect of a deal carefully, and they trust their intuitions about the company and the individuals with whom they're dealing as much as, if not more than, facts and statistics.

And be aware that Spain doesn't have as much of a "telephone culture" as the rest of Europe. Initial contact via phones — or faxes or mail campaigns — won't be particularly effective. Spaniards generally prefer face-to-face meetings, not only with executives but with suppliers as well.

The best way to reassure the Spanish that you're worthy of consideration is to proceed slowly. Lay aside any expectations of a major transaction or contract at the onset of a relationship. Pay a few visits to the company, then initiate a small transaction. Your business dealings will develop commensurately with the growth of your rapport.

The Go-Between

An effective business strategy is to have a mutual friend or connection who can vouch for your reputation and/or personally introduce you to the executives in a company you've targeted. If such an introduction isn't feasible, you can reach your goals alone — by establishing ties based on respect and trust, rather than on monetary gain.

Most foreign enterprises market their products or services in Spain through proficient, trustworthy agents and distributors, most of whom have head offices in Madrid or Barcelona and sub-offices across the country. Another method is to establish a competent subsidiary. Select those who'll represent your company with utmost care, for once you have an association with them, it will be difficult to make a switch. Keep in mind that time devoted to cultivating a good relationship with your agent or distributor is time well spent, as they'll work harder for you. Also, consider hiring legal counsel if you plan to carry out business transactions or set up a subsidiary or branch.

Written Introductions

Written introductions aren't mandatory, but they're helpful. One obtained from a high-level executive in a corporation that conducts business with the one you're interested in or from a close friend of the person you wish to contact will carry a lot of weight. Your reference should write directly to the individual you wish to reach, requesting that he or she give you special consideration.

9 Strategies for Success

Be Patient

Spaniards tend to regard impatience as a character flaw. In meetings, don't try to charge ahead. Allow the host to set the pace. Expect that the first half hour of a meeting will be taken up with chit-chat. Don't try to steer the conversation to business matters in an effort to save time. In decision making, as in negotiations, Spaniards don't rush and they don't like to *be* rushed. Decisions are made at the highest level, so if the key executive isn't present or needs more time to mull things over, a decision won't be handed down.

Be Relaxed About Schedules and Agendas

Spaniards approach schedules, agendas and deadlines in a relaxed manner. Expect delays, last-minute changes in plans, meetings that run over into the next appointment, and conversations that focus on the present, rather than the future. Frequent interruptions during meetings (phone calls, discussions of personal matters) are commonplace.

Avoid Avarice

Refrain from speaking openly about profit making. Spaniard businesspeople are highly competitive and strive for financial reward as much as anyone, but they're discreet about it. And they'll try to reach a fair deal, so that all parties will benefit.

Don't Boast

Though Spaniards are great conversationalists, they hold modesty and understatement in high regard. Little respect is afforded to those who brag about their abilities and accomplishments or about their company's products and services. Let the company's track record speak for itself. On the flip side, never admit to shortcomings or errors as a strategy to win respect. Self-condemnation is viewed as a weakness.

Be a Good Listener & a Good Speaker

Spaniards like to voice their ideas, sometimes repeatedly, loudly and with emotion, and they expect others to listen carefully. They allow others ample opportunity to present *their* ideas — but have no qualms about interrupting (though they dislike being interrupted themselves). Spaniards admire linguistic sophistication, so try to speak as eloquently as possible. In formal settings (such as meetings and negotiations), refrain from making jokes; they often don't translate well across cultures.

Avoid Direct Confrontation

Spaniards have very strong opinions, and they'll usually hold their ground no matter how convincing an opposing argument may seem. They expect others to do the same. Thus, confrontations are bound to crop up. However, they're loathe to engage in *direct* confrontation (such as contradicting or criticizing someone or accusing them of making a mistake), as this shows disrespect and is an assault on the other party's honor. Humiliation caused by direct confrontation may escalate into resentment or anger. Rather than disagreeing or cornering someone verbally, Spaniards will either repeat their own views or offer advice as a means of correcting what they consider to be errors in judgment.

10 Time

Deadlines, Spanish Style

To the Spaniard time is fluid, like the watches in Salvador Dali's famous painting — it can't really be measured, divided or rationed. Spaniards also believe that time exists in great abundance, and so there's enough of it for everything. Time limits, therefore, are seen as artificial and constricting. Deadlines and delivery dates aren't shown the same respect they receive in other cultures.

It's also believed that time works its magic — in business as in wine — and that for ideas to come to their full fruition, they must evolve at their own pace. It's not unusual for the delivery of goods and services to fall behind the schedule previously agreed upon by both parties (though this is less likely to apply to implementation schedules). Quality checks and deadlines that involve many details are apt to be looked on with disdain.

Appointments

Spaniards are adept at juggling several matters at once, and they like to cram many appointments into a day or week. But invariably, they fall behind schedule, as they believe in enjoying what they're doing and so tend to focus intently on the issue at hand. The Spanish don't find this apparent contradiction a cause for despair. As King Juan Carlos I once said, *Yo voy a mi aire* (I go at my own pace).

Perennially Tardy

Since they're often behind schedule, Spaniards are frequently late. Thus, it's commonplace to wait 15 to 30 minutes, or even longer, for a scheduled appointment. (This also applies to social events.) In fact, being on time is more the exception than the rule. That having been said, foreigners should nevertheless arrive at the appointed time in order to convey the seriousness of their intent.

Sometimes Spaniards will stand up the other party with no excuse given. But if a meeting is of vital interest, they'll invariably be punctual. Subordinates don't keep their superiors waiting; to do so would show a lack of respect.

11 Business Meetings

Arranging the Meeting

Business meetings should be scheduled a few weeks in advance, especially if they're with large companies. Don't schedule meetings during *siesta* hours (12:30 to 4:30 P.M.) or during major fiestas. As meetings are formal affairs in Spain, allow yourself enough time to prepare for them thoroughly. And be aware that your Spanish counterparts may choose to conduct the meeting in a restaurant or cafe, rather than in an office. Such informal meetings tend to be impromptu (with participants expected to drop everything to attend) and rather noisy (with everyone talking at once).

It should be noted that the Spanish, who are known for their spontaneity, will sometimes accommodate individuals who call asking for an appointment that same day (because they happen to be in town) or who even just show up at the door. Often, the person who had an appointment months in advance will get "bumped" in order to make a time slot available.

When setting up an initial meeting, try to make contact with the decision makers or with those individuals who have access to them. Oftentimes, senior directors and junior executives are the ones who initiate their company's business relationships, with the top executives being called in later.

If your delegation includes a high-level executive, arrange for him or her to meet the senior persons in the Spanish company, even if it's inconvenient to do so and means changing your itinerary. If you don't, you risk injuring the personal honor of those at the top, and this, in turn, may jeopardize your future business prospects.

Preparing the Spanish for the Meeting

High-level executives in Spain prefer to take control of their calendars rather than to rely on administrative assistants. Thus, assistants may not be able to pinpoint their whereabouts at any given time or remind them of an upcoming meeting. And often, plans and schedules aren't communicated to the lower ranks. In order to alert people to your impending visit (which may minimize delays), it's crucial to confirm your appointment by letter or fax just before your arrival.

Arriving at the Company

Don't be surprised if your meeting is cancelled at the last minute. Either the Spanish have forgotten your appointment, business is backed up, you've been "bumped" in favor of another appointment, or they're not interested in your proposal. Under such circumstances, try not to express disappointment or impatience. Instead, be flexible and willing to meet at a later time, if that seems appropriate.

Small Talk First

Formal greetings and an exchange of handshakes (usually warm and friendly) with everyone in the room are customary at the beginning of a meeting. Then comes about 30 minutes of small talk, which may touch on soccer, travel, world politics, the weather, Spanish cuisine, your trip, and so forth. This is the first step toward establishing a rapport, sizing up your character, and determining whether you're someone worth doing business with.

This social exchange is fundamental to any future business prospects. Those who view such an approach with impatience (in the name of efficiency and "getting to the point") risk being seen as ill-mannered, impudent or even boorish. It's best to allow your host to steer the conversation and set the pace.

Even once the "serious" part of the conversation is under way, digressions may occur. Let them. And be prepared to "read between the lines."

Telling Who's Who

The head of the Spanish team usually guides the conversation, but he'll remain the most reserved and allow his or her subordinates to do the talking. The senior executive will have a greater air of authority and will usually be older than the rest. Subordinates present will show him or her great respect and will wait for direction. They will be careful about what they say and will always defer, so as not to undermine the team leader's authority.

Presenting Your Business

How you state the nature of your business is just as important as *what* you say. Try to speak with as much finesse as possible.

Your presentation should be well-prepared, clear, low-key, and filled with product demonstrations, samples, pamphlets, visuals and thorough explanations. These will stand you in better stead than persuasive arguments. Also, provide detailed information about the price and quality of your products. If the senior executive isn't present, those who are will pass this information on to him in their reports.

Keep in mind that Spaniards aren't concerned with concise, sequential formats. They prefer to discuss each point at length, and they have no qualms about repeating themselves. Once all the details have been covered, conclusions will begin to be drawn. In other words, Spaniards look at the whole picture.

The meeting should end as it began — with handshakes — and, if appropriate, with the exchange of business cards, preferably printed with a Spanish translation on one side and offered with the Spanish side up.

Additional Meeting Guidelines

1. Always gear your presentation to the level of expertise of your audience and their position within the company. Don't inundate them with technical language that they may not understand.
2. Establish team protocol in advance to ensure that questions mistakenly addressed to other team members are deferred to your team leader.
3. Don't show displeasure or impatience toward anyone present. Don't contradict or criticize members of your team in the presence of the Spanish team. Save heated discussions, disagreements and brainstorming for private meetings.

4. If one of your counterparts digresses, don't try to steer them back to the issues at hand.
5. Don't pressure the Spanish to work out all the details on the spot. They like to mull over the facts and figures.
6. Allow the Spaniards to decide when the meeting is over. At the conclusion, your team leader should express thanks for the opportunity to meet. If appropriate, stress your desire to establish a long-term relationship. But keep in mind that this isn't the time to dwell on details and deadlines.

The Language Issue

Since English is the primary foreign language taught in schools and English language proficiency is now critical for professional advancement, many Spanish businesspeople, especially junior-level managers, have a solid knowledge of it. However, be aware that prior to the 1970s, most Spaniards learned French in school. Many do attend English language schools in an effort to keep in step with the times.

Don't praise your Spanish counterparts for their command of a non-Spanish language; such comments will be deemed condescending. (For information on using interpreters, see the next chapter.) You'll have a distinct advantage over your competitors if you translate your presentation materials into Spanish. And any attempt you make to speak Spanish will be met with enthusiasm.

12 Negotiating with the Spanish

In negotiations, several face-to-face meetings are required before the actual decision making even begins. And if you're dealing with middle-level personnel who have limited access to high-level executives, or if the decision maker is unavailable to render a decision, the negotiations will stretch on even longer.

The number of negotiation team members depends on the nature of the business venture and can vary widely. Keep your attorneys out of the negotiating process, as their presence on your team will send a strong message of distrust.

Opening Protocol

After handshakes and casual conversation, a member of the Spanish team will usually introduce each member of the guest delegation to the Spanish senior executive. In most cases, the senior executive will deliver a brief welcoming speech, then turn the floor over to the guest delegation. Spaniards prefer the other side to make their presentation first (thus giving themselves the advantage), though they'll probably have a pretty good idea of their guests' position beforehand.

Your team's main spokesperson should outline your basic points clearly and succinctly. Your team should present a unified front; conflicting statements will be viewed as a weakness. After the guest team has presented its position, the Spanish senior executive will allow his subordinates to respond to specific points, and he will step in to clarify his company's position from time to time.

"Inner Guidance"

Spaniards like to impose their opinions. They're animated, use skillful rhetoric, and have no qualms about resorting to exaggeration and emotion to try to get the opposing team to accept their views. They may interrupt the visiting team (no offense intended), and in disagreement, they may raise their voices (a sign of passionate engagement, rather than anger). They don't change their minds easily — in part because that's considered a sign of weakness. Faced with opposing views, they may restate their original position more emphatically. Most information is processed subjectively (what the Spanish refer to as *duende* or "inner guidance"), and the "hard facts" won't have much impact once an opinion has been formed.

Spanish negotiators are quite conservative. On the whole, they'll choose the path of least risk or the one that promises fewer financial rewards but has a high probability of success. This is because both their power and their public image are on the line. Spanish businesspeople enjoy the negotiating process and they'll take their time resolving any problems that arise. They're quite concerned with negotiating a fair price, and once that price has been determined, they don't take kindly to bargaining.

Ending the Negotiating Session

Don't try to rush the meeting to a close, as this will be interpreted as bullying or impatience. Allow the senior executive on the Spanish side to give his (or her) closing remarks and to field questions. Once he stands up, the session is over. Spaniards demand a formal conclusion, so refrain from last-minute questions or reiterations. The senior executive will shake hands with each member of the visiting team and then leave the room. However, his subordinates will remain behind to chat. Be aware that when a decision is finally made (but prior to the contract being drawn up), specific details will often be lacking.

Interpreters

Conducting business in a language you aren't fluent in puts you at a distinct disadvantage. While hiring an interpreter may be a big expense, it's essential, especially in high-stakes negotiations. Expect the Spaniards to have one as well, unless both sides are fluent in English, Spanish or possibly French. It's not advisable to depend on a member of the Spanish team, since that person, even if he or she has near-native proficiency, will probably not understand all the nuances of your language, and he or she is, after all, on the other side.

Tips on Using Interpreters

1. **Find the Right Interpreter**

Try to find an interpreter who has spent time in your country so that he or she has a complete grasp of subtle nuances and body language. Ideally, you should locate an interpreter in advance of your arrival or bring one with you from your home country. If not, your hotel's business center can refer you to a service that specializes in providing interpreters and translators.

2. The Briefing

Brief your interpreter thoroughly. Provide sample written material for review and explain any specialized vocabulary.

3. Set Up a System

If the other team will rely on your interpreter, and thus he or she will be interpreting both ways (not just from Spanish into your native tongue), you must give the interpreter adequate time to get acquainted with your style of discourse, sense of humor, and body language. Also, it's critical to work out a system that takes into account how long you'll speak before pausing for the interpretation.

4. Don't Exhaust Your Interpreter

Speak in short sentences, make your points crystal clear, and limit each segment to one specific point. Interpreting requires intense concentration, so allow your interpreter to take a rest every two hours. If negotiations continue for longer than a day or if there's a lot at stake, it may be wise to hire two interpreters who work on alternate days or hours. Using an interpreter will stretch a meeting to about three times its normal length, so be patient with the tempo of the discussion.

4. Address the Spanish Team

The Spanish always desire a sense of rapport, so direct your gaze at members of the Spanish team both when you're listening and speaking. Don't look at the interpreter. Some Spaniards are quite proficient in English, and many have at least a foundation in the language, so speak slowly and clearly and avoid idioms and slang.

5. **Take Stock of What's Been Said — Anticipate the Future**

At the close of a meeting or during breaks, review with your interpreter the major points covered. Ask about his or her impression of the other side's position or attitude. Try to determine together the direction the negotiations are taking, and to anticipate points that will have to be introduced or reiterated. This will help your interpreter to convey your desires and intentions effectively.

6. **Drive Home Important Points**

Consider repeating important points, especially in highly abstract and complicated discussions. Make certain that your message and your nonverbal cues are in synch. For example, earnestness should be reflected in the tone of your voice, your facial expressions, and your deportment.

The Spanish Approach to Contracts

Once a verbal agreement has been reached, the next step is to formulate a contract. A Spaniard's word and his handshake were once regarded as sufficient to bind a deal, but no more. While they may not be detail oriented during the initial stages of negotiations, Spaniards prefer contracts that cover every facet of the agreement.

If possible, allow your attorney(s) to handle the minutia of the contract and to interact with the Spanish company's attorneys. But always be present when contracts are actually being drawn up, in case the other side wishes to discuss certain points. Make it clear that while you leave the law to lawyers, you're an interested and active participant in the agreement process, conversant with all of its aspects — in other words, you're not merely a "delegator."

13 Business Outside the Law

The "Black" Economy

After Italy and Greece, Spain has the largest underground or "black" economy in all of Europe. Analysts estimate that at any given time, it encompasses one-fifth of the country's total production of goods and services. High taxes, double-digit unemployment (a whopping 23 percent in 1996, on a par with America at the peak of its Depression Era), and restrictive labor laws (which severely restrict the firing of employees) have been targeted as key causes.

Some analysts assert that Spain's underground economy actually *contributed* to the 1980s boom — by keeping extra cash in consumers' pockets and allowing entrepreneurs to expand their businesses (that is, put more money back into them). They also claim that the underground economy provides many jobs, as well as off-the-record second jobs for those who have trouble making ends meet — thus forestalling political instability and possibly even chaos. Thus, they argue, the black economy has softened the impact of job cuts resulting from the government's implementation of market-oriented economic policies. Still others add that a good percentage of the country's unemployed at any given time are young, first-time job seekers who have the luxury of parental support.

The trafficking of hard drugs escalated after Franco's death. It's estimated that more than half of all South American cocaine passes through Spain, destined for both local consumption and markets throughout Europe. Possession of small amounts of marijuana for "personal use" isn't considered a punishable offense.

Tax Evasion

Historically, tax evasion has been a problem of gigantic proportions. Instances abound of Spanish companies paying part of their employees' salaries in cash so that they don't have to pay as much social security tax. Some companies have declared bankruptcy only to set up operations again without registering — another way of circumventing social security payments. (All companies, including foreign ones, must register to acquire the status of a legal entity.)

Manufacturers sometimes avoid paying taxes by maintaining "flexible" payrolls for people who work in their homes, whom they don't report. Such hidden business operations have accounted for as much as 30 percent of the regional economy of Valencia. Professionals avoid paying taxes by not declaring all of their income, and a good number of Spaniards are engaged in moonlighting (holding a second job in addition to a regular one).

Scandals, Financial & Otherwise

Historically, politics and corruption have gone hand in hand, with the populace tending to look the other way. But occasionally, an invisible line is crossed.

In 1994, a huge scandal rocked the country. It was revealed that the Spanish bank, Banesto, was giving bad loans and making bad investments — a situation made possible by cozy relationships between politicians and financiers, weak bank and stock market regulations, and the insufficient monitoring of bank executives. Another 1994 scandal involved Germany's Volkswagen AG, which alleged that its car-manufacturing subsidiary in Spain had deliberately under-reported losses.

In 1995, when allegations surfaced of government involvement in successful plots to kill Basque terrorists, the bugging of telephones of top-ranking members of society, and other corrupt activities, Spaniards were outraged. Such scandals, augmented by widespread discontent over certain budgetary and reform measures, brought an end to 13 years of PSOE (Spanish Socialist Workers' Party) rule and the presidency of Felipe Gonzalez (who had been re-elected four consecutive times). At the polls, the people cast their votes for the center-right Popular Party led by José María Aznar.

Present Changes – Future Outlook

Prime Minister Aznar asserts that the most effective way to deal with corruption is to improve economic conditions to the point where citizens won't deem it necessary to skirt the law. To that end, his government is laying the groundwork for future tax reforms and for addressing the high unemployment problem. However, it's still to soon to forecast what significant inroads will be made.

14 Names & Greetings

The Intricacies of a Name

On business cards and in correspondence, Spaniards usually list their full name, which consists of a given name followed by a surname (which combines the father's surname and the mother's surname). Thus, if a Spaniard calls himself Francisco Badilla Sánchez, his first name is Francisco, his father's name is Badilla and his mother's name is Sánchez.

Married women don't adopt their husband's surname. Some Spaniards may have double given names, like Spain's Prime Minister Jose María Aznar, Aznar being his father's surname. They may use both their given names or choose to go by the first one only.

In business, the Spanish are quite formal. They usually don't address each other on a first-name basis, even if they're longtime colleagues. Instead, they use each other's professional titles (such as *Profesor*) or *Señor, Señora* or *Señorita,* followed by the paternal surname only. Thus, Francisco Badilla Sánchez would be addressed *Señor* Badilla. Isabel Rodríguez Casco would be called *Señorita* Rodríguez (if she wasn't married). If Isabel married

Francisco, her official name would be Isabel Rodríguez Casco de Sánchez, but she would still be addressed with her father's surname — as *Señora* Rodríguez.

In correspondence, it's respectful to add the title *Don* after *Señor* and *Dona* after *Señora* and *Señorita* and to use the full surname. Thus in a letter, Francisco Badilla Sanchez would be addressed *Señor Don* Badilla Sanchez and his wife, Isabel Rodríguez Casco de Sánchez would be addressed as *Señora Dona* Rodríguez Casco.

Hola, Digame

When Spaniards enter a public space occupied by other people, even strangers (as in an elevator or waiting room), they're expected to extend a general greeting by saying *Hola* (Hello), *Buenos días* or *Buenas tardes* (Good morning or Good afternoon), or *Buenas* for short. Whoever is in earshot is expected to respond in kind, even if they just murmur a reply. Upon leaving occupied public spaces, Spaniards always say *Adiós* (Good-bye). *Encantado* (Pleased to meet you) is somewhat more formal.

If they run into an acquaintance on the street and stop to have a conversation, Spaniards greet each other with *Hola*. However, if they walk past each other without bothering to stop, they say *Adiós,* which in this instance takes on its literal meaning of "Go with God." *Hasta la vista* means "So long, see you soon."

When it comes to telephone protocol, Spaniards often say *Digame*! (Tell me!) in lieu of *Hola,* to which the caller will respond *Oiga*! (Listen) before proceeding with what he or she has to say.

Handshakes, Hugs & Kisses

Spaniards engage in handshaking with far greater frequency than many other cultures. It's common for colleagues within a firm to begin each workday on a handshake and to shake hands when entering and leaving a meeting room — even if they already know the person(s), the conversation is brief, and no agreements were reached. To refrain from shaking hands sends the message that you lack trust.

When eliciting information within the service sector (such as at a bank), conversations between strangers don't commence with a handshake, but they usually end on one. But once a relationship has been established, future meetings will follow the handshake protocol just described.

When it comes to family and friends, Spaniards greet each other with hugs and kisses. Close male friends usually hug or pat each other on the back, and male family members exchange kisses on the cheek. Family and friends greet women and girls with a kiss on each cheek and a slight embrace. Children are taught to offer their cheek for a kiss when greeted by elders, and they adhere to this practice until they're well into their teens.

15 Communication Styles

Spaniards are extremely courteous and formal. Rather than stating a point or opinion directly, they may just offer a few telltale clues, leaving it up to the other parties to deduce their meaning. In many cases, it's difficult for non-Spaniards to ascertain exactly what's meant. It may be helpful to consult privately with one of the Spanish team members (in a business situation) or with a Spanish friend (in a social situation) to find out what message is really being conveyed.

Avoiding "No"

Spaniards abhor direct confrontation (a trait they share with several Asian cultures). They see such behavior as an affront to one's dignity. So they refrain from contradicting or criticizing all but their subordinates, from expressing disagreement overtly, and from saying "No." Instead, they might say, "We'll let you know" or "*Mañana*" (literally, tomorrow, it can mean anything from "later" to "not today" to "sometime in the indeterminate future").

Silence

In some cultures, silence can connote consent, neutrality or even open-mindedness. In Spain, people often remain silent for fear that expressions of their discontent or dissent may be interpreted as criticism, which would then create embarrassment for the other party. And they worry that if they choose an inopportune moment to voice their opinions, they may make themselves or their colleagues look foolish.

Emotionally Volatile

Spaniards aren't fond of contingency plans — alternative modes of action thought out ahead of time in the event that things don't go as originally planned. Too much planning, they believe, leads to a loss of spontaneity. So, when things *do* go awry, Spaniards tend to react emotionally — and that sometimes leads to explosive outbursts. However, they rarely lose their tempers in a business setting, and they expect others to exercise the same control.

16 Customs

Love & Marriage

Under Franco, public displays of affection between the sexes were considered scandalous (*escándalo público*) and grounds for arrest, but nowadays, young lovers are openly affectionate with each other. To a great degree, the Spanish dating game follows the rules found elsewhere in the West, although most seek their parents' approval, and in some rural areas, couples date only if they plan to marry. Engagements tend to last for quite a long time, as couples work to save money for an apartment and furniture before they exchange vows.

Spanish men have a reputation for being extremely romantic and doting during courtship — a pattern that often changes once official vows have been exchanged. Still, with more and more women pursuing careers and advanced studies, husbands are less likely to "rule the roost," especially in urban areas. Weddings usually take place in a Catholic church, even if the bride and groom aren't regular churchgoers; wedding rings are worn on the right hand, rather than on the left, as in many cultures.

As a rule, Spaniards put the preservation of family and stability for their children's sake ahead of their own needs. They expect to encounter bumps along the marital road. Husbands are expected to be unfaithful, and these days, wives are more likely to follow suit than in the past. Divorce is now legal, and divorced women are no longer shunned. Remarriage is common, though in some rural areas, first-time widows wear mourning black for the rest of their lives.

Christmas

Traditionally, Christ's birth was considered much less important than his resurrection, but during the last decade or two, the emphasis has changed. Since the Virgin Mary is Spain's patron saint, the holiday season commences with the feast of the Immaculate Conception (December 8th), which features *los Seisos* (dance of the six) performed by young boys in lavish costumes in front of Seville's Gothic cathedral. The solemn movements of *los Seisos* have been compared to Japanese geisha dances.

As the holiday approaches, towns and cities holds parades featuring *gigantes* — grotesque, towering papier-mache and wood creatures depicting mythological or historical figures. Manned by hidden stilt-walkers, the *gigantes* frolic and dance through the streets spreading good cheer. (They also make appearances at various festivals throughout the year.) Another tradition is for friends to give each other *cestas de Navidad*, willow baskets overflowing with ham, bottles of wine, sugared almonds, marzipan and *turron* (an almond candy that's believed to date back to sacrificial cakes made by the Carthaginians, who came to Spain from Sicily in the 3rd century B.C.). Companies also present these baskets to their employees.

Christmas Eve, called *Noche Buena* or the Good Night, is a time for family reunions and family feasts; the latter may include a whole fish baked with white wine, garlic and tomato; cold almond soup; leg of lamb; and/or a suckling pig roasted in a clay or wood oven. Afterward, everyone makes his way to church for a special midnight Mass known as *Misa del Gallo* (Mass of the Rooster), so-called because it ends in the early hours before dawn, when roosters crow. Christmas Day is for exchanging gifts and for drawing names from an urn (the Urn of Fate) to predict romantic alliances in the coming year. Another tradition is the Day of the Holy Innocents (December 28th), a time for lighting bonfires and playing practical jokes. On New Year's Eve, everyone is given a dozen grapes, which they're expected to swallow for good luck, one at a time, as the clock strikes midnight.

But the most important day of the season is Epiphany (January 6th), which commemorates the coming of the Magi (the Three Wise Men) who, it's believed, rode their camels through Spain. In anticipation of Epiphany (a.k.a. Twelfth Night), Spanish children stuff their shoes with straw or barley for the Wise Men's horses and place them on the windowsill. The most beloved Wise Man of all is Balthazar, for he's the one who carries the gifts for children who've been good. Those who've misbehaved get *caca i carbo* (shit and coal) — the emblems of Hell — though the latter is usually omitted and the former takes the form of brown marzipan lumps, some embellished with spun sugar flies. Families gather to partake of Twelfth Night Cake (*roscón de reyes*), a holiday treat that contains a hidden coin for luck. Many towns reenact the Magi's journey or stage great musical processions on this day.

Holy Week

Religious holidays in Spain involve demonstrations of devotion, but Holy Week (which begins with Palm Sunday) inspires the most spectacular and fervent one of all. On Palm Sunday, the fronds that will be attached to balconies for the remainder of the year are blessed. Later during Holy Week come somber processions of *pasos* (floats) depicting such biblical scenes as the Last Supper, with life-size carved figures covered with hundreds of lit candles and encircled with flowers. The *pasos* are held aloft by hundreds of men who usually belong to various religious brotherhoods. Solemn crowds follow the *pasos* as they move slowly through the streets.

Some of the most dramatic Holy Week processions are held in Seville, where barefoot penitents in pointed black or white hoods trail behind the *pasos*. The only sound heard as the processions go by is the beating of a drum to set the pace. In Catalonia, townspeople reenact the Passion. Some get so involved that more than one person playing Christ has been flogged. Holy Week is also the time of a dramatic pilgrimage to Spain's most famous shrine, Santiago de Compostela; pilgrims come from across the country and across the world to attend.

Fiestas: Fallas, Bulls & Bonfires

Upward of 15 hundred fiestas are held across Spain in any given year. Most cities and towns hold annual ones in honor of their particular patron saint. Activities can include processions, bullfights, soccer matches, fireworks, amusements, dancing and parading in brightly colored regional costumes.

One of the most celebrated fiestas is *Fiesta de San Fermin* (the Running of the Bulls), memorialized by novelist Ernest Hemingway in his novel *The Sun Also Rises*. Held each July in the town of Pamplona, it commemorates a local 3rd-century bishop who's considered the patron saint of bull-fighters; *gigantes* of Normans and Moors frolic in front of Pamplona's cathedral, paying their respects to him. The fiesta's most anticipated event is the *encierro* — the early morning running of six bulls through narrow cobblestone streets to the bullring. Spaniards fill the streets to watch or run alongside; the foolish (and the drunk) sometimes run ahead of the stampeding animals or swat them with rolled-up newspapers. Sometimes the overzealous get caught in the path of the animals and are trampled. In the evening, the bulls meet the matadors, and their fate, in the bullring.

Another internationally famous fiesta is *Las Fallas*, which takes place between March 12th and 18th. The festivities center around papier-mache effigies (*fallas*), some up to 30 feet tall, that satirize politicians, movie stars, athletes and other Spaniards in the media limelight. Some are gruesome, others crude or phallic. Costing millions of *pesetas* and taking many months to build, they're displayed at intersections and town squares. Unlike the *gigantes* (which sometimes date back several generations), *fallas* are designed for burning, and on March 19th, they're ceremoniously set ablaze at midnight. Fireworks follow. The tradition dates back to the Middle Ages, when, in celebration of the summer solstice, Valencian carpenters would burn the wood shavings they'd accumulated during the year in great bonfires.

Gifts

Gift giving is an important facet of both socializing and business. Spaniards receive gifts from family and friends on both their birthdays and their saint's days. In business, gifts are generally presented at follow-up meetings (never at a first meeting) after a rapport has been established. Select a gift that's meaningful but that doesn't suggest any kind of hidden agenda. For instance, unless the gift is of very high quality (like a fine pen), it shouldn't sport your company's logo; otherwise, your offer will be considered insincere and an attempt at self-promotion. Gifts should always be wrapped beautifully.

If you're invited to a Spaniard's house for dinner, it's good form to send or bring a gift such as wine, chocolate or flowers. (Avoid chrysanthemums and dahlias, as they're associated with death, and bouquets or arrangements of 13 flowers, as these are considered bad luck.) Candy is appropriate for children.

On occasion, a Spanish host will present his guests with gifts. These should be opened at once as a show of courtesy and gratitude. Be aware that praising a Spaniards' possessions (a scarf, a pen) may result in the owner feeling obligated to give it to the admirer as a gift.

17 Dress & Appearance

A Passion for Fashion

Spaniards wear the finest quality clothing they can afford, in an effort to convey high social standing and affluence. And they try to keep in step with the latest fashion. Even Spanish children and teenagers seem to put a lot of thought into choosing what they wear. They're always neat in appearance, and their socks match their sweaters as a rule.

Not surprisingly, Spaniards pay a lot of attention to the care of their garments. Once home from work or school, they change right away into more casual wear. However, when it comes time for the evening meal, many dress up again, regardless of whether they're dining at home or in a restaurant.

In some ways, Spanish dress is more relaxed than it was even a decade ago. Cathedrals and churches no longer require women to wear sleeved dresses and men to wear ties. And the farther west you travel, the less attention people pay to fashion.

In the Workplace

Corporate attire is quite formal and conservative. Men wear finely tailored suits in dark colors (European styles predominate) and expensive but refined accessories. Black shoes are essential. Name brands are the most popular, and Spaniards are adept at spotting them and evaluating their worth. Women are expected to dress conservatively, in subdued colors, but with a little more flair than their male counterparts. Dresses and skirts are considered more appropriate than pant suits, both at work and when going out in the evening.

Ethnic Attire

Ethnic costumes, which vary greatly from region to region, are donned for festivals and sometimes for weddings. But even in everyday life, some wear a traditional accessory such as a beret (Basque men), a cloth cap (Galician men), or a bright kerchief (Aragonese women).

18 Reading the Spanish

Honor and Honra

Honor is such a critical concept to the Spanish that they have two words for it: *honor* and *honra*. *Honor* is virtue or a good name, while *honra* is a sense of personal honor, dignity or self-esteem. The Spanish go to great lengths to avoid shame and preserve *honor,* as it is a kind of currency that enables them and their families to move in society. This emphasis on honor sometimes leads them to interpret an action or remark as an insult where none was intended. ("If I die, I'll forgive you. If I live, we'll see," goes one Spanish saying.) *Honra,* in contrast, is indestructible, for it's a manner or approach to life.

Gestures and Expressions

- Though handshakes often prevail, the Spanish are fond of kissing one another on both cheeks, both for greetings and departures — even when meeting someone for the first time. This applies to women kissing women, men kissing women, and in recent years, more and more men kissing men.

- Always maintain eye contact in conversation. Avoiding it may be interpreted as dishonesty. "Snapping" eyes are an indication of impatience or anger.
- The Spanish gesticulate constantly, so they think it odd to keep one's hands in one's pockets during a conversation.
- Spaniards beckon to one another by stretching out their arm and making a scratching motion with their hand, palm down.
- To emphasize a point, Spaniards snap their hand down as if pounding on a table.
- Joining the tip of the forefinger and the tip of the thumb to form a circle, a gesture that means "okay" in the U.S., is considered obscene.
- Beware of the "thumb's up" sign. It can mean support for the Basque separatist movement and may infuriate some people.
- It's considered unladylike for women to cross their legs at the knee while sitting, but it's customary for men to do so.
- Yawning or stretching in formal situations is socially unacceptable.
- Sneezes are greeted with *Jesus*, the equivalent of *Bless you*.
- Though Spaniards tend not to smile, this doesn't necessary reflect their state of mind.
- The closer Spaniards stand to you, the more they're exhibiting familiarity and trust.

19 Entertaining

The first time a Spaniard invites you to his or her house for dinner, it's common practice to decline, as the invitation may simply be a display of politeness and respect. However, if the individual insists or extends another invitation at a later date, than the invitation is sincere and it's appropriate to accept. Spaniards consider their homes to be private sanctuaries. Therefore, such invitations are an honor and shouldn't be taken lightly.

If it's a dinner where business will be discussed, Spaniards generally prefer to have it at a favorite restaurant where they're familiar with the food and the wine list. Most restaurants serve from 1 or 2 P.M. until 4 P.M. and then in the evening from 8 P.M. to 11:30 P.M. But in summer, especially in the larger cities, many restaurants and bars remain open until the crack of dawn.

Traditional Fare: More Than Just Paella

Spaniards are epicures at heart, and gastronomy is taken very seriously. In fact, one of the earliest known cookbooks was written by a Spaniard named Diego Granado Maldonado and published in Madrid in 1609. (It carried the elaborate title *Libro del arte de cozina, en el qual se contiene el modo de guisar de comer en qual quier tiempo, assi de carne, come de pescado ... assie de pasteles, tortas y salsas ...*) Though fast-food chains like McDonald's, Burger King and Wendy's have opened their doors in major Spanish cities, it's hard to imagine such enterprises winning over local hearts and stomachs.

A typical *desayuno* (Spanish breakfast) consists of strong expresso or thick hot chocolate and *bollos* (rolls) with jam or *churros* (sugar-coated crullers). Expresso is available straight (*café solo*), with a little milk (*café cortado*), with a lot of milk (*café con leche*), or laced with brandy (*carajillo*). Weaker coffee is called *café americano* (thought to suit the tame American palate). Few Spaniards drink tea (*té*). One of the most famous places for *churros* in all of Spain is Madrid's centuries-old Churrería de San Gines, where a line for the tasty fritters usually starts to form at about 4 A.M. Some *Madrileños* stop here on their way home after a long night of partying.

The most important meal of the day is *la comida,* which begins around 2:30 in the afternoon during siesta. Soup (such as *gazpacho,* a spicy vegetable soup served cold, or *sopa de ajo,* garlic soup), salad or another appetizer usually precedes the main dish.

Each region has its own classic dishes, but pork, ham, fish, chicken, sausages made of lamb, rice and legumes predominate. Potatoes, peppers, eggplant, tomatoes, olives, garlic, anchovies and olive oil are culinary staples. Seafood (including hake, scallops, octopus, oysters, trout, crayfish and crab) is a northern specialty, as is game (wild boar, goat). Squid, which is sometimes batter-fried, sometimes grilled or sauteéd in a sauce, also makes a frequent appearance on Spanish tables. One Catalonian town holds a green onion festival in March; another is home to a snail-eating feast in early May. Basque dishes include *porrusalda* (a soup of chicken, potatoes and leeks), *caldo Gallego* (a white bean soup), *callos a la Vasca* (tripe), and *rabo encendido* (simmered oxtail).

Many foreigners consider *paella* — a saffron-enhanced rice dish adorned with a combination of shellfish, chicken, rabbit, snails and / or vegetables — Spain's national dish, though it was first prepared only about a century ago. In fact, the country's most traditional dish may be *cocido*, a chickpea stew fortified with potatoes, carrots, cabbage, meats and sausages. *Cocido* is served in three courses, first the broth, then the vegetables, and lastly the meats, which are sometimes shredded together. In Catalonia, *cocido* includes beans, and in Andalusia, it may be embellished with pears and squash. *Tortilla española* is a sublime omelette made with potatoes, onions, salt and olive oil.

At around 5 or 6 in the evening, Spaniards partake of *merienda*, a between-meal snack usually consisting of a tart or pastry. *Cena*, the evening meal, is much lighter than *la comida* and is usually eaten between 8 P.M. and midnight. Spaniards are apt to skip dessert, but when they indulge, it's usually in fruit and cheese, rice pudding or *flan* (custard).

Vino is Divino

Spain boasts more vineyards per square kilometer than any other country in the world, and thus wine accompanies many a meal. The sherries of Andalusia (particularly from the Jerez region) are the country's most celebrated wines; they range from pale and dry to dark-hued and sugary. The dry *manzanilla* and *fino* and the medium *amontillado* sherries are aperitifs, while the sweeter *olorosos* and cream sherries are dessert wines. Castile-León, Catalonia and Basque Country also have distinguished wine regions. Spaniards favor reds from the region of La Rioja; the best of these are labeled *Reserva* and *Gran Reserva*. Wine drinks include *sangria* (red wine, fizzy lemonade, sugar and chopped fruit) and *agua de Valencia* (a sparkling wine called *cava* mixed with orange juice).

Orujo is a popular after-dinner liqueur. Made primarily in Galicia, it resembles Italian *grappa* and is usually served cold. Some regions produce a lovely drink known as *yerbas* (herbs), made of various local herbs steeped in an anisette base.

Dining Etiquette

- It's considered polite to seat and serve women and older people first.
- Guests of honor are seated at the host's right.
- During the meal, hands should be kept clearly visible at all times, never in the lap.
- Spaniards adhere to the continental style — fork in the left hand and knife in the right. The utensils should never be switched.
- Silverware isn't used to eat sandwiches, pizza or fruit (unless the fruit is served sliced).
- Lay the knife and fork side by side across the plate to indicate that you're finished. Crossing the utensils or positioning them on opposite sides of the plate sends the message that you wish to have more.
- Leaving food on your plate, especially at a dinner party in someone's home, may insult the host.
- It's considered polite to compliment the host at a dinner party or the waiters in a restaurant.

- The proper way to beckon a waiter in a restaurant is to raise your hand. Spaniards may summon the waiter by saying "Psst," but tourists who do this are considered somewhat ill-mannered.
- Spaniards remain enthusiastic smokers, despite strong legislation to the contrary.

Tapas Bars

At any hour of the afternoon or evening, urban Spaniards (especially *Madridileños*) visit *tapas* bars — also called *tascas, tabernas bares, mesones* or *bodegas. Tapas* (sometimes referred to as *pinchos*) are appetizer-size dishes; most establishments prepare a wide variety to choose from. Many will be on display; others will be listed on a chalkboard. Typical fare includes *chorizo* (garlic sausage), *queso manchego* (sheep's cheese from La Mancha), *patatas bravas* (potatoes in a picante tomato sauce), *calamares fritos* (fried squid), olives, sautéed shrimp, and *jamón serrano* (salt-cured ham dried in mountain air). These are often consumed while standing up at the bar or at little tables in the back and washed down with sherry.

Spaniards often make an evening of going from bar to bar in search of the best *tapas*, a custom called the *chateo*. Waiters often don't keep track of orders; when you're ready for the check, they'll ask what you had or simply count up the number of empty toothpicks to arrive at the bill.

The Check and Tipping

Restaurant waiters won't bring the check (*la cuenta)* to the table until it's requested. (It's customary to pay the waiter.) In most establishments, a service charge (*servicio*) is factored in; nonetheless, it's common practice to leave a small tip — 5 to 10 percent of the bill. (Urban taxi drivers also get 5 to 10 percent. Hotel desk clerks and doormen are tipped 100 *ptas*, while porters receive 50 *ptas* per suitcase, and maids 200 *ptas* per week.)

If a Spaniard invites you for a snack or a meal, he has every intention of paying the bill. Don't mention that you wish to "repay" your host. And never suggest splitting the bill. "Going Dutch" is considered very bad form, and you may earn a reputation for being a "tight wad." Just reciprocate at a latter date, and make certain to choose a fine restaurant.

The generosity of Spaniards is boundless; they often pay the bill for strangers with whom they've struck up conversations in bars and restaurants. And when they dine in large groups, they usually argue about who gets the pleasure of paying, rather than trying to figure out who owes what, down to the last *peseta*.

20 Socializing

Bullfighting: Ancient Tradition & National Obsession

Bullfighting *(la corrida* or *corrida de toros)* isn't considered a sport (the bull never wins) but rather a powerfully moving art form, a ballet of highly stylized movements that tests the courage, daring, grace and finesse of the matador and the stamina and cunning of the bull. It symbolizes the supremacy of man over beast, the rational over the instinctual. In many ways, it appeals to what Spanish philosopher and writer Miguel de Unamuno called his country's "tragic sense of life."

Spectacles with bulls date back to ancient Crete and imperial Rome. As they grew in popularity, crumbling Roman amphitheaters in Seville, Cordova, Toledo, Cadiz and elsewhere were rebuilt and embellished to accommodate them.

Every *corrida* begins with a grand procession led by one or two mounted *alguaciles* (bailiffs in 16th-century costume) and features three matadors (*toreros*) who face two bulls each. The matador — dressed in a richly embroidered silk jacket and waistcoat called a *traje de luces* (suit of lights) —

incites the bull to charge by waving red capes. Then a picador, astride a horse, stabs the bull in the neck and shoulders, and the banderillo puts barbed darts in the bull's shoulders. The kill is done *al volapié* (fleet-footedly) or *recibiendo* (with the matador standing still and receiving the bull). Either way, it's accomplished with a single thrust of a sword over the horns. (The meat is sold the next day at the local butcher shop.)

Today, only about 200 matadors are qualified to kill a bull. Those who excel in the ring may be awarded the bull's ear(s) or tail, carried through the main door of the ring on the crowd's shoulders, and esteemed as national champions. But if the matador exhibits cowardice, cannot bring the bull to a halt for the kill, or makes a bloody mess, the bull may be led from the ring alive and the matador bombarded with derisive whistling, a shower of seat cushions from the stands, and searing criticism in the press.

The first book to explain *corrida de toros* "both emotionally and practically," in Spanish or any other language, was Ernest Hemingway's *Death in the Afternoon,* published in 1932. Hemingway's *The Dangerous Summer,* written 27 years later, chronicles his friendship with matador Antonio Ordoñez.

Manolete, who was gored to death in 1947, is considered one of the greatest matadors who ever lived. Among the more unusual matadors to gain recognition in Spain have been "Billy" Bong Way Wong, a first-generation Chinese-American known as "El Chino," and, more recently, Cristina Sánchez, the only woman to reach the top echelon for several decades. (Women bullfighters first appeared in the ring at the end of the 19th century and were treated as curiosities. At the time, several untalented male matadors were caught disguising themselves as women in an attempt to garner attention.)

The larger stadiums can seat 20,000. The most expensive seats are in the shaded front rows, the least expensive in the sunny back rows. The bullfight is one event for which Spaniards are never late. Bullfighting season extends from about April to early November, and bullfights are usually held one or two days a week; in some regions, they're held only during fiestas. The most celebrated *corridas* (such as at Madrid's San Isidro Festival) are televised nationally.

In the early 1980s, the popularity of *corridas* seemed in serious decline, but thanks to brash young matadors like Jesulin de Ubrique — whose all-female audiences are known to hurl their underwear into the ring — a record 16,500 *corridas* took place in 1996, with some 37,000 bulls meeting their demise.

Fútbol

Fútbol (soccer), introduced by the British in the late 19th century, is the country's favorite spectator sport, with even more aficionados than bullfighting. Even small villages have at least one playing field. Thanks to the nationalistic tug-of-war between Castile and Catalonia (and Franco's passion for the game), a rivalry arose between the F. C. Barcelona and Real Madrid teams many decades ago. To this day, all Spaniards have a preference for one of the two, even if they follow a third.

Tickets to matches are sold at stadiums, which seat up to 120,000, although for big matches (which are televised nationally), they can be secured at ticket agencies. A recent craze is indoor soccer (*fútbol sala*), often played in large underground car parks.

When Spain won a silver medal in basketball at the 1984 Olympics, the popularity of that sport increased manyfold. King Juan Carlos loves to sail, ski, hunt and fish. But *fútbol* remains the country's Number One favorite.

Jai Alai: A Basque Tradition

Also known as *pelota,* jai alai dates back to the medieval French game of *jeu de paume* which, in 1530, was declared the exclusive perogative of the nobility. The earliest mention of a Basque playing it was in the 15th century, when King Henry VII awarded 100 pounds sterling to a Basque player whose prowess he admired. Cervantes, in one of his stories, made the hero a *pilotari* (pelota player), and a proverb of that era — *aun esta la pelota en el tejado,* fickle as a ball rolling off a roof — suggests that the game was popular enough to have entered the common culture.

It wasn't until 1912 that the game's rules were codified. In 1924, jai alai was included in the Olympic Games in Paris. Today, the game even has an official patron saint, a 16th-century Jesuit — Basque, of course — whose skeletal right hand shows the telltale deformation of someone who, in life, was a *pilotari.*

Flamenco: A Gypsy Legacy

This passionate and highly popular musical tradition combines guitar playing, staccato hand clapping (*palmada*), clinking castanets, dancing and passionate singing. Female dancers wear bright dresses with close-fitting bodices, frilled skirts and trains; male dancers wear snug suits with short jackets, wide hats and boots.

Flamenco (literally, Flemish) was created by Andalusian gypsies in the late 18th century. One 19th-century account describes a tall gypsy girl dancing "with charming lissomness and grace. Her bare feet lightly touched the ground on which pebbles were strewn, as though she were dancing on a carpet" as the tempo continued to increase. Beginning in the 1950s, flamenco was exploited for its tourist appeal as a typically Spanish art form. Inevitably standards fell — until in 1977, when they were restored by dance/choreographer Antonio Gades, who took charge of Spain's first permanent flamenco/classical dance company.

Nowadays, flamenco is performed by professionals in flamenco clubs across the country. But flamenco-style folk dances (*sevillanas)* are executed by all who wish to partake, and they remain popular despite the post-Franco invasion of rock n' roll and U.S. pop music.

Lotteries and Gambling

Spaniards believe in *suerte* (luck) more than most Europeans, so it's no surprise that they're passionate about games of chance. Many try to beat the odds in a half dozen lotteries, as well as in soccer pools. Lottery tickets are sold at booths on many street corners, and vendors stroll through restaurants and bars with reams of tickets in hand. The biggest lottery of the year is the centuries-old *El Gordo* (the Fat One), held on December 22. Entrants have a chance to win about US$1.2 billion in prizes, along with a jackpot that averages US$235 million. Across the country, millions watch on television as the orphans of Madrid's San Ildefonso School select the winning numbers.

Casinos are also an obsession, and they can be found in many regions. Most are equipped with restaurants and discotheques. Mallorca's casino even has a tennis club and an adjoining beach. In most such establishments, a jacket and tie are advised or required, and foreigners must bring their passports to the table.

Conversational Taboos

Some personal information, readily exchanged in other cultures, is viewed as intensely private in Spain. Spaniards don't openly discuss their family life or religious beliefs — or their jobs. It's not unusual to know a Spaniard for quite some time and still be unaware of what he or she does for a living. Intimate topics are never broached with acquaintances or coworkers; they're reserved for discussion behind closed doors with family and very close friends.

Safe topics in casual conversation include sports, travel, food, culture and history (but avoid broaching the Spanish Civil War or Spain's neutrality during World War II).

Topics to avoid at all costs are high taxes, unemployment and religion. Politics is touchy. It's all right to discuss bullfighting, but know that many Spaniards will take any criticism of the spectacle to heart.

21 Basic Spanish Phrases

English	Spanish
Yes No	*Si* *No*
Good morning Good afternoon Good evening Hello	*Buenas días* *Buenad tardes* *Buenas noches* *Hola*
Good-bye	*Adiós*
Please	*Por favor*
Thank you (very much)	*(Muchas) gracias*
You're welcome	*De nada*
Excuse me; I'm sorry	*Pardón*
My name is _____	*Me llamo* ______
I don't understand	*No comprendo*
Do you speak English?	*Hablan inglés?*
See you tomorrow	*Hasta mañana*

22 Correspondence

Postal delivery in some parts of the country can be slow. One reason is that the number of postmen assigned to a particular area is determined by the number of registered residents, and many foreigners prefer not to register.

In general, the order of information in a mailing address is as follows:

Sr. Don
Jorge Hidalgo de Caviedes
El Mundo
Calle Serrano, 61
28002 MADRID

The most common word for "street" is *calle*, but there's also *avenida* and *paseo* (both major streets), *callejon* (a small street), and *plaza* (a square). If a street is short, the buildings may not be numbered, and *s/n* (*sin número,* without number) will be written instead.

Dates

The date is typically written numerically, with the day followed by the month and the year abbreviated. Thus May 30, 1997 becomes 30/5/97.

23 Useful Telephone Numbers

These are local numbers in Spain. If dialing from outside Spain, dial your country's international access code, followed by Spain's country code [34].

- International access code from Spain 07
- Long Distance Access Code 9
- City Codes: Madrid (1), Barcelona (3), Seville (5), Valencia (6), Granada (58), Pamplona (48)
- Local Operator 009
- Directory Assistance 003
- Police Emergency: municipal 091, national 092
- Ambulance: Madrid 061 or (91) 522 22 22, Barcelona 061 or (93) 300 20 20, Seville (95) 435 01 35
- Fire (Madrid, Barcelona, Seville) 080
- 24-Hour Pharmacy (Madrid) 098
- State Railroad: Madrid (91) 328 90 20, Barcelona (93) 490 02 02, Seville (95) 454 02 02
- Iberia, Binter, Aviaco & Viva Airlines
  . . . . Domestic (901) 33 31 11
  . . . . International (901) 33 32 22

24 Books & Internet Addresses

Travelers' Tales: Spain, edited by Lucy McCauley. Travelers' Tales, Inc., San Francisco, California, USA, 1995. Diverse, first-person accounts offer a tantalizing look at Spanish culture.

Spain: The Root and the Flower, by John A. Crow. University of California Press, Berkeley, California, USA, 1985. A fascinating exploration of Spain and its inhabitants, from the country's earliest beginnings to the post-Franco era.

The New Spaniards, by John Hooper. Penguin Books, London, England, 1995. An indepth look at Spain's transformation from a dictatorship to a democracy, as well as insightful commentary on the Spain of the 1990s.

Business and Democracy in Spain, by Robert E. Martinez. Praeger, Westport, Connecticut, USA, 1993. A detailed study of such issues as business and European integration, business and labor, the relationship between employers and workers, and the restructuring of the economy in the 1990s.

Barcelona, by Robert Hughes. Alfred A. Knopf, New York, USA, 1992. The dramatic, 1500-year history of Barcelona by an award-winning art critic and historian.

The Mezuzah in the Madonna's Foot, by Trudi Alexy. Simon & Schuster, New York, USA, 1993. Oral histories exploring 500 years in the paradoxical relationship between Spain and the Jews.

Bury Me Standing: The Gypsies & Their Journey, by Isabel Fonseca. Alfred A. Knopf, New York, USA, 1995. An insightful, first-hand look at the gypsies of Bulgaria, Poland, the Czech Republic, Slovakia and elsewhere in Eastern Europe.

Internet Addresses

The Webfoot's Guide to Spain

http://www.webfoot.com/travel/guides/spain/spain.html

Tuspain

http://tuspain.com/

EUNet Spain (in Spanish)

http://www.eunet.es/

Info About Spain

http://donde.uji.es/listados/about_spain.html

Go Spain

http://www.clark.net/pub/jumpsam/gospain.shtml

WWW Sites in Spain

http://www.publired.es/guia/www_i.htm

Spain Online

http://www.spainonline.com/